PROMPT ENGINEERING : THE ART OF ASKING

MASTER GENERATIVE AI TOOLS LIKE CHATGPT & MIDJOURNEY

YASWANTH SAI PALAGHAT

To all of you who have followed my content on social media, thank you for your support and encouragement. Your belief in my work has been a source of inspiration and motivation for me, and I am grateful for the opportunity to share my ideas with you.

I would also like to thank all of you who supported my previous three books, "The Door To Financial Freedom", "The Art Of Unleashing Your Potential" & "The Money Stories". Your kind words and positive feedback were truly appreciated, and I hope that this book will provide even more value and guidance to you on your journey toward success and fulfillment.

Finally, I want to express my deep gratitude to all of the people who have helped me along the way, including my friends, family, colleagues, and mentors. Your support and guidance have been invaluable, and I am forever grateful for all that you have done for me.

With heartfelt thanks, Yaswanth Sai Palaghat

Contents

Contents

Foreword

In a world where the resonance of artificial intelligence is echoing in every corner, understanding and leveraging its vast potential are skills of utmost importance. **'Prompt Engineering: The Art of Asking'** serves as a beacon of guidance for those navigating this exciting landscape, providing a much-needed perspective on the nuances of interacting with AI.

This book is the culmination of countless experiences, trial and error, and the relentless pursuit to master one of the key aspects of AI engagement - prompt engineering. It is about learning the art of asking the right questions, shaping the course of AI-driven dialogues, and harnessing the power of AI to your advantage. Whether you are an enthusiast, a seasoned programmer, a digital marketer, or a content creator, this book will enrich you with practical insights and methodologies.

The knowledge contained in this book is much more than a skill. It is a toolset, a unique perspective, a game-changer that can open up endless possibilities in your journey with AI. From enhancing personal productivity tools to scaling up a business, prompt engineering can determine how efficiently you harness AI.

As you turn these pages, you will find much more than just 'how-tos'. This book will introduce you to the mindset required to frame effective prompts, help you understand the subtleties of AI interactions, and offer practical techniques you can apply immediately.

In 'Prompt Engineering: The Art of Asking,' Yaswanth Sai Palaghat takes you on a transformative journey. It's not just about interacting with an AI; it's about becoming a better problem-solver, a more effective communicator, and gaining a competitive edge in this AI-driven world.

Don't miss out on this opportunity to uncover the art and science of prompt engineering. Embrace this journey, and see how this powerful skill can redefine your AI interactions.

So, get ready to flip the page and enter the fascinating world of prompt engineering. Happy reading!

Preface

The inspiration to write "Prompt Engineering: The Art of Asking" came from my own journey as a content creator and digital marketer in the ever-evolving technological landscape. While grappling with artificial intelligence tools, I realized that the heart of every effective AI interaction lies in the prompt - the questions we ask, the tasks we set, and the direction we provide to the AI.

However, prompt engineering isn't just about formulating a command or query. It's about understanding the complex dance between human curiosity and machine intelligence. It's about refining our questions to extract the best possible answers and results from AI models. And most importantly, it's about enhancing our ability to communicate, reason, and solve problems.

This book is a compilation of all the knowledge, insights, and practical techniques I've gained along the way. While writing it, I aimed to keep it as accessible, relevant, and useful as possible, regardless of the reader's background. Whether you're a tech enthusiast, a professional, or someone simply looking to enhance their interactions with AI tools, this book has something valuable for you.

"Prompt Engineering: The Art of Asking" isn't just a guide; it's an invitation to explore and experiment. As you traverse through the chapters, you'll be equipped with practical strategies, intriguing perspectives, and a whole new understanding of AI interactions. But beyond all of that, I hope this book inspires you to ask better questions, not just to AI, but in all areas of life. After all, it's through questions that we understand, learn, and grow.

I'm grateful for the opportunity to share this journey with you, and I'm eager to see how these strategies will transform your interactions with AI. Let's dive in and uncover the art of asking together.

Yaswanth Sai Palaghat

CHAPTER ONE

Unmasking AI: A Broad Overview

Welcome to the world of Artificial Intelligence (AI) - a field that combines computer science, data analysis, machine learning, and many more disciplines to simulate human intelligence processes by machines, especially computer systems. It has undeniably become a significant part of our everyday lives, whether we realize it or not.

From recommendations on our favorite streaming platforms to the digital assistants on our smartphones, AI surrounds us. It's enhancing business processes, aiding in scientific research, powering innovative applications, and even making our homes smarter.

AI operates on various principles and methodologies. It's essential to understand that AI isn't a monolithic entity, but an umbrella term encompassing several different technologies, including Machine Learning (ML), Deep Learning (DL), Neural Networks, Natural Language Processing (NLP), and more. Each of these fields has its unique mechanisms, applications, and potential.

Machine Learning, for instance, allows machines to learn from data and make predictions or decisions without being explicitly programmed to perform the task. Deep

Learning, a subset of ML, uses artificial neural networks to mimic the workings of the human brain, enabling the machine to learn from large amounts of data.

On the other hand, Natural Language Processing enables machines to understand and respond to human language, powering applications like virtual assistants, translation tools, and chatbots.

The real magic happens when these technologies work in tandem, leading to innovative applications like generative AI models, which will be the main focus of our journey in this book.

As we move forward, we'll dive deeper into these fascinating aspects of AI, with a special emphasis on language models and their applications. This chapter has set the stage for our exploration, providing you with a fundamental understanding of the AI landscape. Let's dive into the specifics in the next chapter and unravel the marvels of language models, the cornerstone of tools like GPT-3, GPT-4, and ChatGPT.

CHAPTER TWO

Language Models Unveiled: An Introduction to Generative AI

Language Models (LMs) are the heart of many AI applications, from voice assistants like Siri and Alexa to autocorrect features on our smartphones. LMs are designed to predict the likelihood of a sequence of words appearing in a sentence, paragraph, or document. This capability allows them to generate human-like text, giving rise to a class of AI known as Generative AI.

Generative AI takes creativity to a new level. It's all about models that can generate content - be it a poem, a piece of music, an image, or a piece of code. When it comes to text, these models, often called Generative Language Models, can create entire paragraphs, making them sound as if a human wrote them. One prime example of a generative language model is ChatGPT, developed by OpenAI.

The underpinning of these language models is a type of neural network architecture known as Transformers. These models learn patterns in the input data, understand context, and can generate human-like text. They are trained on vast amounts of text data, learning grammar, facts about the world, reasoning abilities, and even some biases from the data they are trained on.

One fascinating feature of these models is their ability to perform "few-shot learning". This means they can learn to perform a new task with just a few examples. You can prompt them to generate a poem, write an essay, answer questions, and they can often do a decent job.

However, it's important to understand that while these models are powerful, they don't "understand" text in the way humans do. They are pattern matches of extraordinary scale, learning to predict the next word in a sentence based on the patterns they've seen in the training data.

In the next chapters, we'll explore how we can interact with these models effectively using prompts and the way we frame our commands or questions. We'll also look at different types of prompts and how to optimize them for better results. So, let's delve deeper into the exciting world of Prompt Engineering.

CHAPTER THREE

Decoding the Language Model: The Heart of Chatbots

So, what's a **language model?** And how does it power the chatbots that we interact with regularly? In this chapter, we delve into these fundamental questions, breaking down the intricacies of how language models work and their role in the creation of conversational AI.

At its core, a language model is an AI model that understands, generates, and works with human language. It's a model trained on a vast corpus of text data, learning the nuances of language syntax, semantics, and context through the process.

Language models predict the likelihood of a word or a sequence of words appearing in a sentence. For instance, given the words **"I am feeling very,"** the language model could predict that the next word might be **"happy," "tired," "hungry,"** or any other probable word. The ability of language models to predict and generate text forms the foundation of chatbots.

Chatbots, particularly those powered by sophisticated language models like GPT-3, leverage this predictive ability to engage in detailed, human-like conversations. When you provide input to a chatbot, it uses the language model to predict an appropriate response based on what it has learned during its training.

However, it's crucial to note that while these language models can generate incredibly human-like text, they don't truly **"understand"** the text in the same way humans do. They're essentially pattern-matching systems that leverage statistical associations to produce responses. They can't reason, don't possess consciousness, and don't hold opinions, even though their outputs might give such an impression.

In the next chapter, we'll introduce the concept of **prompt engineering**, which essentially involves crafting our inputs to these chatbots in a way that directs them toward the output we desire. You'll discover the art of formulating prompts that lead to more useful, accurate, and engaging responses from AI-powered chatbots. Buckle up, because this is where the real adventure begins!

CHAPTER FOUR

Prompt Engineering: The Art of Communicating with AI

Now that we've laid the groundwork by understanding AI and language models, it's time to dive into the heart of our exploration - **Prompt Engineering**. If AI and language models are the vehicles that carry us toward the future, prompt engineering is the steering wheel that guides their direction.

So, what exactly is prompt engineering? It's the process of crafting inputs (prompts) in a way that guides AI models, especially language models, to produce desired outputs. It's not just about asking questions or giving commands to an AI; it's about how you frame these questions and commands to get meaningful and useful results.

Think of **prompt engineering** as the art of having a successful conversation with an AI. Just like in human interactions, the way you frame your prompts significantly affects the kind of response you get. But unlike human interactions, AIs don't infer unspoken context or interpret prompts beyond their learned patterns. Therefore, being clear, precise, and contextually relevant becomes even more crucial in AI interactions.

Prompt engineering might seem straightforward, but there's an art and science to it. You'll need to understand the subtleties of the AI model you're dealing with, grasp the influence of the prompt's structure, tone, and context, and learn to iterate and refine your prompts for better outcomes.

The subsequent chapters will dive deeper, uncovering different types of prompts and exploring how to optimize them to maximize results across different scenarios - from learning and brainstorming to specialized prompts for tools like **ChatGPT** and **Midjourney**.

Prepare yourself for an exciting journey into the art of asking - the key to unlocking the full potential of AI!

CHAPTER FIVE

Types of Prompts: Unveiling the Spectrum

Prompts are more than mere questions or commands. They are gateways through which we shape our interactions with AI. By understanding the different types of prompts, we can become better **'prompt engineers'**, leading to more efficient and effective AI interactions.

Prompts can generally be categorized into a few different types, each with its unique characteristics and applications:

1. **Descriptive Prompts:** These prompts are used when you need the AI to generate content in a certain style or manner. They are often used in creative tasks like writing a story, generating a poem, or creating a script. For example, <u>**"Write a short horror story set in a haunted mansion."**</u>

2. **Instructive Prompts:** These prompts are directive in nature and often require a specific output from the AI. They are straightforward, asking the AI to perform a task or answer a question. For example, <u>**"Translate the following English text to French."**</u>

3. **Exploratory Prompts:** These prompts are used when the objective is to explore a concept or idea with the AI. They are ideal for brainstorming sessions or when seeking diverse perspectives on a topic. For example, <u>**"What could be the potential impacts of AI in education?"**</u>

4. **Dialogic Prompts:** These prompts are typically used when interacting with conversational AI, like chatbots. They involve posing a question or a statement that encourages a back-and-forth interaction. For example, <u>**"Tell me more about the history of artificial intelligence."**</u>

Understanding these categories can enhance our ability to communicate effectively with AI models. It allows us to choose the most appropriate type of prompt based on our specific needs and goals, thereby maximizing the quality and usefulness of the AI's response.

In the upcoming chapters, we'll dive deeper into each of these prompt types, exploring their nuances, and understanding how to use them effectively in various scenarios. We'll also discover how to optimize them for better results, making this knowledge an indispensable part of your AI toolbox.

CHAPTER SIX

The Golden Rules of Prompt Engineering

Mastering the art of prompt engineering is about more than knowing the types of prompts. It's about understanding and applying certain guiding principles or 'golden rules' that can enhance the quality and relevance of the AI responses. Here are some key rules to keep in mind:

1. **Be Clear and Specific:** AI, despite its advanced capabilities, doesn't possess human-like understanding. Therefore, clarity and specificity are crucial. The more specific your prompt, the less room there is for AI to generate off-topic or irrelevant responses.
2. **Provide Context:** AI models like GPT-3 don't have the memory of past prompts or external world knowledge beyond their training data cut-off. So, for complex interactions, provide the necessary context within the prompt.
3. **Prompt Length Matters:** While it's important to provide sufficient detail, extremely long prompts can cause the AI to lose focus. Try to strike a balance between brevity and completeness.

4. **Experiment and Iterate:** Not all prompts will work perfectly the first time. Don't be afraid to experiment, iterate, and refine your prompts. It's through this process of trial and error that you'll learn what works best for a given scenario.

5. **Use the AI's Training Data to Your Advantage:** Language models are trained on vast amounts of data and can generate content in various styles. If you want a legal document, you can ask it to <u>**"Write as a lawyer would."**</u> If you want a simplified explanation of a concept, you can prompt it to <u>**"Explain it like I'm five."**</u> Leveraging the diversity of the AI's training data can greatly enhance your results.

6. **Set Output Format:** If you're looking for a specific format in the output, specify it in the prompt. Whether you want a bullet-point list, a detailed paragraph, or a numbered sequence, make it clear in your instruction.

These rules provide a robust framework for crafting effective prompts. However, they aren't absolute or exhaustive. Different situations may require different approaches. As we explore different types of prompts and their applications in the following chapters, you'll see these rules in action and discover how flexible and dynamic the art of prompt engineering can be.

Remember, the essence of prompt engineering lies not only in asking the right questions but also in understanding how to ask them. Let's continue our journey to unravel this fascinating skill further.

CHAPTER SEVEN

Priming the Pump: Basic Prompting Techniques

Before we delve into the complexities of different types of prompts and their uses, it's essential to start with the basics. Basic prompting is about crafting simple and straightforward prompts to achieve desired outputs. It serves as the foundation upon which more complex prompt engineering skills can be built.

A basic prompt usually involves a direct command or question. For example, if you're using a language model like GPT-3 and you want it to generate a poem, a basic prompt might be: **"Write a poem about spring."** Or if you're using a chatbot for information, you could prompt: **"Tell me about the history of the internet."**

While basic, these prompts give us an introduction to how AI models respond to our commands or queries. Here are a few tips for effective basic prompting:

1. **Be Direct:** Ensure your prompt is direct and to the point. Ambiguity can lead to off-topic or undesired

outputs.

2. **Define the Task Clearly:** Make sure the AI understands what you're asking. If you want a story, specify it. If you need an explanation, make it clear.
3. **Use Proper Language Structure:** As language models learn from structured data, they respond better to well-structured prompts.

However, basic prompting may not always get you the perfect output. There may be instances where the response from the AI is not quite what you expected. This is where our journey into more advanced types of prompts begins. In the following chapters, we will explore different categories of prompts that help us enhance the quality and relevancy of AI outputs.

So, while basic prompting may be our starting point, remember, this is just the tip of the iceberg!

CHAPTER EIGHT

Mastering AI Responses: Understanding the Echo of Your Prompts

As we continue our exploration into prompt engineering, it's essential to understand that it's not just about what we say to the AI, but also how we interpret its responses. A significant part of prompt engineering is learning to make sense of the AI's output, and, where necessary, refining our prompts to get better results.

The AI's responses, or 'echoes' of your prompts, can tell you a lot about how well your prompts are working. Are you getting the information or output you wanted? Is the AI going off on tangents or giving irrelevant responses? These are indicators of how effective your prompts are.

Here are some strategies to help you master AI responses:

1. **Be Adaptable:** If the AI isn't giving you the output you want, don't be afraid to change your approach.

Experiment with different ways of framing your prompt or providing more (or less) information to guide the AI.

2. **Iterate and Refine:** Sometimes, getting the desired output requires several iterations. Take note of what works and what doesn't, and use this knowledge to refine your prompts.

3. **Understand AI's Limitations:** AI models don't have personal experiences or beliefs, they generate outputs based on patterns they've learned from the data. They don't understand context the way humans do, and they can't access real-time or proprietary information. Understanding these limitations can help you shape more effective prompts and interpret responses correctly.

4. **Read Between the Lines:** AI's responses often need to be interpreted with care. Look for underlying patterns or recurring themes that might give you insights into how the AI is processing your prompts.

5. **Learn from Mistakes:** Not every response will be a home run, and that's okay. Mistakes or 'failures' can be valuable learning opportunities. Analyze them to understand what went wrong and how you can improve.

Remember, prompt engineering isn't a one-way street. It's an ongoing dialogue with the AI, where the inputs and outputs continually inform and shape each other. With practice and patience, you'll become adept at navigating this conversation, leading to more fruitful interactions with AI.

CHAPTER NINE

AI as a Learning Companion: Crafting Prompts for Knowledge Acquisition

One of the most powerful applications of AI lies in its potential to aid our learning journeys. Generative AI models can transform the way we acquire knowledge, acting as interactive companions that cater to our unique learning styles and pace. However, unlocking this potential requires an understanding of how to craft effective learning prompts.

1. **Clarifying Concepts:** AI can be a great tool to break down complex concepts. The key is to ask direct, specific questions. For example, <u>"Explain quantum computing in simple terms."</u>
2. **Deep Dives:** If you're interested in a detailed exploration of a topic, prompt the AI to provide comprehensive information. For instance, <u>"Give me a detailed overview of the history of artificial</u>

<u>intelligence."</u>

3. **Examples and Applications:** Learning can be enhanced by understanding real-world applications and examples. For instance, <u>"Provide examples of how machine learning is used in healthcare."</u>

4. **Comparisons:** AI can help clarify your understanding by comparing two or more concepts. For instance, <u>"Compare and contrast supervised and unsupervised learning in machine learning."</u>

5. **Quizzes and Reinforcement:** AI can help reinforce your learning by creating quizzes or summary reviews of the topics learned. For example, <u>"Create a five-question quiz on the key principles of blockchain technology."</u>

Remember, AI doesn't replace traditional learning methods but augments them. It offers a personalized, interactive learning experience that can enhance understanding, stimulate curiosity, and make learning more engaging. As we progress through this book, we'll continue exploring how to harness the power of AI through effective prompt engineering. Stay tuned!

CHAPTER TEN

Thinking Out of the Box: Brainstorming Prompts for AI

Artificial Intelligence can be a powerful ally in brainstorming sessions. It offers the potential to generate diverse ideas, perspectives, and solutions, thereby enriching the creative process. However, harnessing this potential requires careful prompt engineering.

Here are some strategies for crafting effective prompts for brainstorming:

1. **Ask Open-Ended Questions:** Encourage expansive thinking by posing open-ended questions. Instead of asking, **"Should we use solar energy?"** you might ask, **"What are some innovative ways we could use solar energy?"**

2. **Request Multiple Ideas:** Ask the AI to generate multiple ideas or solutions to a problem. This can provide a broader range of options to consider. For example, **"List ten unique marketing strategies for an online education platform."**

3. **Seek Diverse Perspectives:** Request the AI to think from different perspectives. For instance, <u>**"What might be some potential challenges of AI technology from an ethical, economic, and technical standpoint?"**</u>
4. **Combine Concepts:** Invite the AI to blend different concepts to generate novel ideas. For instance, <u>**"How might we incorporate gamification into an e-learning platform?"**</u>
5. **Use Visualisation Prompts:** Asking the AI to describe a future scenario can also stimulate creative thinking. For example, **"Describe a day in the life of a city fully powered by renewable energy."**

Remember, brainstorming is about the quantity and diversity of ideas, not their immediate feasibility. The goal is to generate a wide array of options, which can later be refined and assessed for practicality. AI can significantly aid this process if we learn to ask the right questions. As we move forward, we will explore more specific applications of prompt engineering, so stay tuned!

CHAPTER ELEVEN

Becoming Fluent in ChatGPT: Tailoring Prompts for Specific AI Tools

Every AI tool has its unique characteristics and functionalities. As a language model developed by OpenAI, ChatGPT has specific features and nuances that make it distinct. To fully leverage its capabilities, it's crucial to understand how to tailor your prompts specifically for this tool.

Here are some strategies to help you become fluent in ChatGPT:

1. **Direct Instructions:** ChatGPT responds well to clear, direct instructions. Be explicit about the format and content you want. For instance, **"Write a short, suspenseful story set in a haunted house."**

2. **System Messages:** You can use system messages, which are instructions for the model that aren't part of the conversation. This can be useful to set the behavior of

the AI at the start of the conversation.

3. **Temperature and Max Tokens:** You can control the randomness (temperature) and length (max tokens) of the output. A higher temperature will make the output more random, while lower values make it more deterministic. Adjusting these settings can help tailor the output to your needs.

4. **Experiment and Iterate:** Different prompts and settings can lead to varied results. Don't be afraid to experiment, iterate, and learn from unsuccessful attempts.

5. **Stay Informed:** OpenAI regularly updates and improves its models. Keep up to date with these changes to make the most of the tool.

Remember, becoming fluent in an AI tool like ChatGPT is a process. It takes time, practice, and a willingness to learn and adapt. As you gain experience, you'll develop a better sense of which prompts work best and how to adjust your approach to get the results you want. In the coming chapters, we'll continue to explore how to tailor prompts for other specific AI tools. Stay tuned!

CHAPTER TWELVE

A Picture is Worth a Thousand Words: Guiding AI to Generate Images with Text

The intersection of AI and creativity expands beyond just text. With recent advancements in AI, we can now use text prompts to guide AI in generating images. These tools, like Midjourney, have opened up new horizons of creative expression and problem-solving.

However, just like with text generation, effective use of these tools requires carefully crafted prompts. Here are some strategies to guide AI in generating images with text:

1. **Be Explicit:** Clearly describe the elements you want in the image. Instead of saying <u>"Draw a bird"</u>, say <u>"Draw a bird with green feathers and a yellow beak sitting on a branch"</u>.

2. **Specify Style and Mood:** You can guide the AI in generating images with a particular style or mood. For instance, <u>"Create an image of a bustling city street in</u>

<u>the style of an impressionist painting"</u>.

3. **Visual Metaphors:** AI can interpret and visualize metaphors. For example, **<u>"Create an image of time flying"</u>.**

4. **Experiment:** The results can be unpredictable, so don't be afraid to try different prompt styles and explore the possibilities.

5. **Iterate and Refine:** You might not get the perfect image on your first try. Refine your prompts based on the outputs and iterate.

Remember, AI image generation is not about perfect replication of reality, but about opening new creative pathways. It's a tool that can bring the wildest of your imaginations to life, provided you learn to ask in the right way. As we dive deeper, we'll further explore how you can harness the power of AI for various applications through effective prompt engineering.

CHAPTER THIRTEEN

Unlocking Midjourney: Prompt Crafting for AI Text-to-Image Tools

In the realm of AI text-to-image translation, Midjourney is a significant player. This tool, renowned for its ability to transform descriptive language into striking visuals, opens up uncharted territories for creativity. However, to utilize its potential to the fullest, understanding the art of prompt crafting specific to Midjourney is essential.

1. **Understanding Midjourney's Unique Flavor:** Midjourney, as an AI tool, has its own idiosyncrasies. Understand its stylistic tendencies, the sort of imagery it leans towards, and how it interprets different types of prompts.

2. **Play with Abstractions:** While it's important to be specific when you want a precise image, Midjourney also allows room for abstract prompts. Phrases like **"the texture of a dream"** or **"the color of silence"** can yield surprisingly intriguing results.

3. **Visual Puns and Metaphors:** Midjourney tends to do well with visual metaphors and puns. Try prompts like <u>**"a clock made of sand"**</u> or <u>**"a fish with a city skyline for scales."**</u>

4. **Iterative Prompting:** Sometimes, getting the image you want may require an iterative process. You may start with a broad concept and then narrow down based on the AI's output, refining and tweaking your prompt in a back-and-forth interaction.

5. **Unexpected Combinations:** Midjourney can be great at generating surreal images that combine unrelated objects or concepts. Try out prompts like <u>**"a knight chess piece with skyscrapers as its castle".**</u>

Remember, working with Midjourney is a dance between guiding the AI with your creative intent and embracing the unexpected outcomes that the AI brings to the table. With practice and a sense of adventure, you'll soon be orchestrating this dance to create visuals that push the boundaries of imagination.

CHAPTER FOURTEEN

MidJourney Prompts Guide

Midjourney Prompts are short text phrases that the Midjourney bot interprets to generate images. The bot breaks down the words and phrases in a prompt into smaller pieces, called tokens, which are compared to its training data to generate an image. Crafting a well-thought-out prompt can help create unique and exciting images.

There are two types of prompts: Basic and Advanced.

- **Basic Prompts** can be as simple as a single word, phrase, or emoji. The Midjourney Bot works best with simple, short sentences that describe what you want to see. For instance, instead of a long list of requests like "Show me a picture of lots of blooming California poppies, make them bright, vibrant orange, and draw them in an illustrated style with colored pencils", a more effective prompt would be "Bright orange California poppies drawn with colored pencils".
- **Advanced Prompts** can include one or more image URLs, multiple text phrases, and one or more parameters. Image URLs can be added to a prompt to influence the style and content of the finished result.

Parameters can change how an image generates, including aspect ratios, models, upscale, and more.

When crafting prompts, it's important to note:

1. **Prompt Length:** Short prompts will rely heavily on Midjourney's default style, so a more descriptive prompt is better for a unique look. However, super-long prompts aren't always better. Concentrate on the main concepts you want to create.
2. **Grammar:** The Midjourney Bot does not understand grammar, sentence structure, or words like humans. Word choice matters and more specific synonyms often work better. Fewer words mean each word has a more powerful influence.
3. **Focus on What You Want:** It is better to describe what you want instead of what you don't want. If you want to ensure an object is not in the final image, try advance prompting using the **"--no"** parameter.
4. **Think About What Details Matter:** Be as specific or vague as you want, but anything you leave out will be randomized. Being vague is a great way to get variety, but you may not get the specific details you want.
5. **Use Collective Nouns:** Plural words leave a lot to chance. Try specific numbers. **"Three cats"** is more specific than **"cats."** Collective nouns also work, **"flock of birds"** instead of **"birds."**

Remember, a well-crafted prompt can help make unique and exciting images with the Midjourney Bot.

CHAPTER FIFTEEN

MidJourney Advanced Prompts

Midjourney is an excellent tool for those who may not have artistic skills but possess a vivid imagination. It allows users to generate high-quality, unique images based on their text prompts. The more descriptive the prompt, the more vibrant and unique the output. For instance, a prompt like "a cowboy wearing a tuxedo on the moon" will generate an image that matches that description.

However, beyond the raw prompt text, there are advanced options that can be used to create more predictable and consistent image outputs. Here are some of the ways you can generate variations in images and some of the advanced settings for the same:

1. **Providing Keywords - 'Style':** Mentioning the design or genre name in the prompt, like s<u>tandard, Japanese anime, bloodborne, steampunk, Pixar movie, Waterhouse, cyberpunk,</u> and more. You can also specify the name of the artist as your style, such as <u>**Da Vinci, Picasso, Salvador Dali, Andy Warhol,**</u> and more.

2. **Stylize:** You can specify some numbers in the setting in a format <u>**– -s <some number>**</u>, showing low and high

stylize options.

3. **Chaos:** Represents the abstraction of the image. It is also written in the same format as the stylized output like _ -chaos 70_. The number can vary from 0 to 100, where 0 is low abstraction while 100 is high abstraction.

4. **Resolution:** To get a high-resolution image, you need to specify its resolution by mentioning the image quality keywords like 4K, 8K, ultra-detailed, ultra photoreal, intricate details, and more.

5. **Aspect Ratio:** The aspect ratio is a major parameter in producing images. You can specify the image ratio as **width: length(Example: use ar 16:9 at the end of any prompt for thumbnails).** If you do not mention the aspect ratio in the prompt, it will produce an image with a default aspect ratio (1:1).

6. **Passing an Image as a Prompt as URL:** If you want an image similar to an image available online but with consistent outputs, you can use the page URL of the image.

7. **Applying Weights to the Image Prompts:** You can even specify the number of images you want and also the weight in your image prompt.

8. **Weights to the Word Prompts:** You can specify the weightage for each word in your prompt to influence the output.

9. **Filtering Out Words from Images:** If you want to discard any extra item or some picture inside the image that you think looks bad, you can use the **"- -no"** keyword to remove that object from your image.

Midjourney also offers a **"/describe"** command that lets users upload any image that gives them a set of four text prompts as an output. The output of this command describes the image that you have uploaded. And you can use those prompts to generate unique images.

There are also several Midjourney prompt generator tools available, such as Hugging Face, Midjourney Prompt Helper, Midjourney Prompt Builder, Future Tools, and even ChatGPT, which can help you generate the right prompt for your image.

CHAPTER SIXTEEN

The Art of the Ask: Crafting Compelling Conversational Prompts

Conversations form the foundation of human interaction and communication, and with AI like ChatGPT, we can now extend that realm into the digital world. To craft compelling conversational prompts that spark engaging AI interactions, here are some strategies:

1. **Open-ended Questions:** Open-ended questions stimulate more elaborate responses and invite AI to provide more comprehensive answers. For instance, <u>**"What are the potential impacts of AI on society?"**</u> as opposed to <u>**"Is AI impacting society?"**</u>

2. **Building Dialogue:** To have an engaging conversation, make your dialogue organic. Respond to the AI's output and build upon it. Remember that a conversation is not just a series of disconnected questions; it's a flow of interconnected ideas.

3. **Contextual Prompts:** Provide context to guide the conversation. For example, <u>"Imagine you are a historian from the year 2100. Describe how you would interpret the impact of AI on the early 21st century."</u>

4. **Challenging Assumptions:** Push the AI's capacity for complex reasoning by posing questions that challenge assumptions, <u>"What if AI had never been invented? How might our lives be different?"</u>

5. **Being Patient:** Good conversations often take time to build. Don't rush. Let the conversation unfold naturally.

Mastering the art of the ask is about more than just getting answers. It's about engaging in a dynamic exchange of ideas, pushing boundaries, and exploring new territories of thought. In the next chapters, we will explore how to apply these principles to specific areas like learning, and creative writing. Stay tuned!

CHAPTER SEVENTEEN

Context Matters: Influence of Contextual Information on Prompt Response

Context plays a crucial role in shaping the responses generated by AI. By manipulating the context of your prompts, you can steer the AI in different directions and obtain diverse responses. Here's how contextual information influences prompt response:

1. **Explicit Context:** Direct instructions included in your prompts provide the immediate context that the AI uses to generate its response. For instance, if you say, **"Write a poem about autumn,"** the AI will use **"autumn"** as the context for the poem.

2. **Implicit Context:** This refers to the broader, unspoken context that the AI takes into account when generating responses. For example, if you're discussing a historical event, the AI uses its pre-training knowledge about that period to inform its responses.

3. **Conversation History:** The AI takes into account the entire conversation history up to a certain limit. It uses this history to maintain the context and continuity of the conversation.

4. **System Messages:** These are special types of context that set the behavior of the AI at the start of the conversation.

5. **Contextual Ambiguity:** Sometimes, prompts can be ambiguous, and the AI has to make a guess based on the context. For instance, the word "**bank**" could mean a financial institution or a riverside. The AI uses the surrounding context to determine the intended meaning.

Understanding the role of context in AI responses allows you to craft more effective prompts and anticipate how the AI might interpret them. As we go further, we'll delve into how to leverage this knowledge for different applications like brainstorming, learning, and creative writing. Stay tuned!

CHAPTER EIGHTEEN

The Importance of Precision and Clarity in Prompts

Precision and clarity in prompts are fundamental when interacting with AI. Without a clear directive, AI might produce vague or off-target responses. On the other hand, a carefully crafted, precise prompt can yield rich and insightful results. Here's why precision and clarity matter:

1. **Avoiding Ambiguity:** AI can misinterpret vague or ambiguous prompts. By being precise and clear, you can minimize misinterpretations and guide the AI toward your desired outcome. For example, instead of <u>"Tell me about the climate,"</u> ask <u>"Describe the climate in Paris during summer."</u>

2. **Controlling Scope:** A clear and precise prompt helps control the scope of the response. For instance, <u>"Explain the basics of quantum computing"</u> will generate a general introduction, while <u>"Explain how quantum superposition contributes to the power of quantum computing"</u> will yield a more focused

response.

3. **Influencing Depth:** The precision of your prompt can influence the depth of the response. If you want a deep, thorough response, a precise prompt like <u>**"Discuss the impact of Shakespeare's works on modern literature"**</u> will serve better than a generic <u>"Discuss Shakespeare."</u>

4. **Steering the AI's Style:** You can also use precise prompts to influence the AI's writing style. A prompt like <u>**"Write a detailed report on climate change"**</u> will yield a more formal and informational tone, while <u>**"Tell me a story about a world affected by climate change"**</u> will lead to a more narrative and imaginative response.

Learning to craft precise and clear prompts is akin to learning a new language—the language of AI interaction. By mastering this, you can unlock the full potential of AI tools and use them to your advantage, whether it's for learning, brainstorming, creative writing, or any other application you can imagine. Stay tuned for more insights and strategies in the following chapters!

CHAPTER NINETEEN

The Subtleties of Prompt Refinement: From Good to Great

Good prompts get the job done, but great prompts inspire AI to produce exceptional results. The process of refining prompts is a delicate art, balancing clarity, creativity, and direction. Here are some strategies for refining your prompts:

1. **Iterative Refinement:** After receiving an AI response, rework your prompt based on what worked and what didn't. This iterative process can often lead to better results over time. It's an experimental journey of learning and adapting.

2. **Nuance and Detail:** Adding more detail or nuances to your prompts can often guide the AI to provide richer responses. For example, instead of <u>**"Write a sci-fi story,"**</u> try <u>**"Write a sci-fi story set on a sentient spaceship journeying through a quantum portal."**</u>

3. **Explicit Instruction:** Sometimes, it's helpful to instruct the AI on the format or structure you want the output

to follow. For example, **"Write a dialogue between two characters arguing about the ethics of AI,"** will help guide the format of the AI's response.

4. **Limiting Scope:** Refining your prompts may involve limiting the scope of your question to get a more focused response. Instead of **"Tell me about the French Revolution,"** you might ask, **"Describe the role of the bourgeoisie in the French Revolution."**

5. **Experimentation:** Experiment with different phrasings, styles, and approaches. Sometimes a change in perspective or a new way of asking the question can yield dramatically different responses.

Remember, refining prompts isn't just about improving AI responses; it's also about enhancing your understanding and fluency in this new language of human-AI interaction. As you gain proficiency, you'll be better equipped to leverage AI tools for various applications. Stay tuned as we continue exploring the intricate world of prompt engineering!

CHAPTER TWENTY

Decoding AI Errors: How to Learn from Misfires

AI, like all tools, is not perfect. It can make errors, misunderstand prompts, or generate unexpected outputs. These misfires, while initially frustrating, can be incredibly instructive. Here's how you can learn from them:

1. **Spotting the Error:** Understanding when the AI has misinterpreted your prompt is the first step. This requires a clear understanding of your expectations from the prompt and an ability to critically evaluate the AI's response.

2. **Understanding the Error:** Once an error is spotted, try to understand why it happened. Did the AI misunderstand the context? Did it extrapolate in a direction you didn't anticipate? Reflecting on these questions can provide valuable insights.

3. **Refining the Prompt:** Use the insights gained from understanding the error to refine your prompt. Make your instructions clearer, specify the context better, or

ask the question differently.

4. **Learning from Patterns:** Over time, you might notice patterns in the types of errors the AI makes. Maybe it consistently struggles with certain kinds of prompts or contexts. These patterns can provide clues for how to improve your prompts in the future.

5. **Iterative Learning:** Like all learning, understanding AI errors is an iterative process. Each misfire is an opportunity to learn and improve.

Learning from AI misfires is a crucial part of prompt engineering. It's through these errors that we can gain deeper insights into how AI thinks, allowing us to craft better prompts and achieve more accurate results. So, embrace these AI misfires, learn from them, and use them to hone your skills in the art of prompt engineering. Stay tuned for the next chapter, where we'll delve into advanced techniques for specific applications!

CHAPTER TWENTY-ONE

The Future of Prompt Engineering: The Next 5 Years

As we look forward, the art of prompt engineering will continue to evolve and play a crucial role in human-AI interaction. Let's explore the possible developments in the next five years:

1. **Increasing Precision:** As AI improves, we'll likely see an increase in the precision of responses to our prompts. This means your prompts will yield even more specific and relevant results.
2. **Understanding Nuance:** AI will get better at picking up on the nuances in our prompts, leading to richer and more detailed responses.
3. **Better Contextual Understanding:** AI will improve its ability to understand the broader context of prompts. This will lead to more accurate and coherent responses.
4. **Active Learning:** Future AI may have the ability to learn actively from the prompts, refining its understanding and responses as the conversation progresses. This

might result in a more dynamic and adaptable conversation experience.

5. **More Natural Conversations:** We'll likely see improvements in AI's ability to maintain the flow of the conversation, making interactions feel more natural and engaging.

6. **Prompts Beyond Text:** AI might evolve to understand and respond to prompts in other formats, like images, sound, or even abstract concepts. This will vastly expand the scope of human-AI interaction.

7. **Ethical Guidelines for Prompt Engineering:** As the impact of AI grows, we may also see the development of ethical guidelines for prompt engineering to prevent misuse and ensure AI benefits all of humanity.

The future of prompt engineering is bright, filled with opportunities and advancements. As we continue to navigate this landscape, remember that the essence of prompt engineering remains the same: it's the art of asking—the art of sparking curiosity, pushing boundaries, and seeking answers. And as we move into the final chapter of this book, remember that this journey of learning and discovery is just beginning. Stay curious, stay excited, and stay tuned!

CHAPTER TWENTY-TWO

Creating a Symphony with AI: The Art of Continual Learning and Improvement

Interacting effectively with AI, particularly through prompt engineering, is not a static skill; it's a dynamic, ever-evolving process. Like conducting a symphony, it requires finesse, adaptation, and continual learning. Here's how you can sustain this process:

1. **Embrace the Learning Curve:** There will be a learning curve as you understand how to interact with AI effectively. Don't be discouraged by initial difficulties. Instead, treat them as opportunities to learn and improve.

2. **Continual Experimentation:** Keep experimenting with different types of prompts and observe the AI's responses. Learn from both the hits and misses.

3. **Stay Updated:** AI technology is rapidly advancing. Make an effort to stay updated with the latest improvements

and changes. These developments may introduce new possibilities for prompt engineering.

4. **Share and Learn:** Engage with the community of AI enthusiasts and professionals. Share your insights, learn from their experiences, and collaborate on new ideas.

5. **Think Creatively:** Prompt engineering is as much an art as it is a science. Use your creativity to come up with unique prompts and to explore unconventional uses of AI.

6. **Ethical Considerations:** As you refine your skills, keep in mind the ethical implications of your work. Ensure your interactions with AI contribute positively to society and respect the principles of fairness, privacy, and accountability.

Prompt engineering is a journey, not a destination. It's a continual process of learning, experimenting, and adapting. As we close this book, remember: the key to mastering this art lies not in achieving a perfect understanding, but in embracing the process of continual exploration and improvement. Enjoy the symphony!

CHAPTER TWENTY-THREE

Bonus: Prompt Templates

Just like a skilled artist has a palette of colors, a prompt engineer should have a collection of effective prompts at their disposal. This final section serves as a practical toolkit for your prompt engineering journey. It contains a wide array of versatile prompt templates divided into five distinct categories: Learning, Work, Brainstorming, Roleplay, and Text to Image prompts.

Whether you're looking to understand a complex concept, navigate a work situation, spark creativity, engage in a dynamic roleplay, or guide AI in generating compelling visuals, there's a prompt template here for you. Consider these not just as static examples, but as starting points for developing your unique style of prompt crafting. Happy engineering!

Learning Prompts

1. "Explain the concept of {Concept Name} like I'm five."
2. "What are the key principles of {Subject}?"
3. "Discuss the historical context of {Event}."

4. "Compare and contrast {Topic A} and {Topic B}."
5. "Provide a detailed summary of {Book/Article}."
6. "What are the implications of {Study/Research Findings}?"
7. "Can you teach me how to do {Task/Skill}?"
8. "What is the current state of research on {Topic}?"
9. "Who are the key thinkers in {Field} and what are their contributions?"
10. "Describe the process of {Procedure/Method} step by step."

Work Prompts

1. "Generate an agenda for a team meeting about {Project/Topic}."
2. "Write a project proposal for {Project Idea}."
3. "Draft an email explaining {Situation/Problem} to a client."
4. "Brainstorm marketing ideas for {Product/Service}."
5. "Create a SWOT analysis for {Company/Project}."
6. "Outline a project plan for {Project Name}."
7. "Compose a performance review for an employee who {Employee Performance Description}."
8. "Give me talking points for a negotiation about {Topic/Issue}."
9. "Draft a response to a customer complaint about {Customer Complaint}."
10. "Create a sales pitch for {Product/Service}."

Brainstorming Prompts

1. "List out innovative ways to solve {Problem}."
2. "What are some potential names for a {Product/Service} that does {Function}?"
3. "Generate ideas for blog posts about {Topic}."
4. "What are different ways to market {Product/Service}?"
5. "Think of unique themes for an {Event/Project}."
6. "What are some creative uses for {Product/Item}?"
7. "Imagine the future of {Field/Industry}. What does it look like?"
8. "List potential improvements for {Product/Service}."
9. "What are different strategies for increasing customer engagement?"
10. "Come up with plot ideas for a sci-fi novel."

Roleplay Prompts

1. "Play the role of a customer service agent handling a complaint about {Issue}."
2. "Roleplay as {Historical Figure} and describe their perspective on {Event/Issue}."
3. "Imagine you are a salesperson trying to sell {Product}. How would you pitch it?"
4. "Play the role of a detective solving a mystery. Start with finding the clues."
5. "Roleplay a counseling session about {Personal Issue}."
6. "Take on the role of a tour guide introducing a visitor to {Place}."

7. "Roleplay a negotiation between a business owner and a supplier."
8. "Act as a Java Developer and take a mock interview with me for the Java Developer role"
9. "Play the role of an astronaut describing the view of Earth from space."
10. "Imagine you are a book critic reviewing {Book Title}."

Text to Image Prompts

1. "Visualize a serene mountain landscape at sunrise."
2. "Create an image of a bustling cityscape in the future."
3. "Imagine a mystical forest filled with magical creatures."
4. "Visualize a space station orbiting a distant alien planet."
5. "Create an image of a medieval castle under siege."
6. "Imagine an underwater city, teeming with aquatic life."
7. "Visualize a scene from the Victorian era."
8. "Create an image of a quiet, cozy cabin in the winter."
9. "Imagine a climactic battle scene in a fantasy world."
10. "Visualize a peaceful garden full of blooming flowers."

Coding and Technology Prompts

1. "Explain the basics of Python programming."
2. "What are the principles of good software design?"
3. "Create a guide to understanding machine learning."
4. "What are some tips for effective debugging?"
5. "Discuss the importance of data security and privacy in today's world."

6. "How can I learn to code if I'm a complete beginner?"
7. "What are the key differences between SQL and NoSQL databases?"
8. "What is the role of artificial intelligence in healthcare?"
9. "How does blockchain technology work?"
10. "What are some exciting trends in tech to watch for?"

Personal Development Prompts

1. "What are the habits of highly successful people in {field}?"
2. "How can I improve my time management skills?"
3. "Give me a step-by-step guide to developing emotional intelligence."
4. "List some effective stress management techniques."
5. "What are the principles of mindful living?"
6. "Suggest a plan to build self-confidence."
7. "How can I improve my public speaking skills?"
8. "Provide tips for successful goal setting."
9. "What is the importance of a growth mindset?"
10. "Outline a 30-day plan for developing a new habit."

Philosophy and Psychology Prompts

1. "Explain the concept of self in existential philosophy."
2. "What are the primary schools of thought in psychology?"
3. "Discuss the theories of {Philosopher}."

4. "What are some notable experiments in social psychology?"
5. "Explain the concept of mindfulness from a psychological perspective."
6. "Discuss the role of nature vs. nurture in human development."
7. "What are some critiques of Freud's theories?"
8. "How does cognitive behavioral therapy work?"
9. "What is stoicism and how can it be applied in daily life?"
10. "Discuss the concept of happiness from a philosophical perspective."

Fitness and Health Prompts

1. "What are the fundamentals of a healthy diet?"
2. "How can I incorporate exercise into my daily routine?"
3. "List some effective exercises for full-body strength."
4. "What are the benefits of yoga and meditation?"
5. "Create a beginner's guide to mindfulness-based stress reduction."
6. "Outline a 30-day beginner's running plan."
7. "What are some easy home workouts?"
8. "Give me a weekly meal plan for a balanced diet."
9. "Explain the science behind intermittent fasting."
10. "List some mental health self-care practices."

Cooking and Nutrition Prompts

1. "Create a recipe for a healthy breakfast smoothie."
2. "How can I cook a perfect medium-rare steak?"
3. "What are some nutritious lunch options for kids?"
4. "Give me a list of pantry essentials for a home cook."
5. "Create a three-course meal plan for a romantic dinner at home."
6. "Explain the process of making sourdough bread."
7. "List some creative ways to use avocados in cooking."
8. "What are some easy and quick dinner recipes?"
9. "How to make homemade pasta?"
10. "What are the nutritional benefits of quinoa?"

Writing and Creativity Prompts

1. "How can I overcome writer's block?"
2. "Give me a prompt for a suspenseful short story."
3. "What are some techniques for developing engaging characters?"
4. "Generate an outline for a blog post on {topic}."
5. "List some creative writing exercises to improve my writing skills."
6. "Create a plot twist for a mystery novel."
7. "How can I make my writing more descriptive?"
8. "Give me a writing prompt that involves time travel."
9. "What are some tips for writing compelling dialogues?"
10. "Create a world-building guide for a fantasy novel."

Travel and Adventure Prompts

1. "List some must-visit places in {Country/City}."
2. "What are some tips for budget traveling?"
3. "Describe a day in the life of a local in {Country/City}."
4. "What are some adventure sports to try in {Place}?"
5. "List essential items to pack for a beach vacation."
6. "Give me a food guide for {Country/City}."
7. "Describe the cultural significance of {Landmark}."
8. "What are some off-the-beaten-path destinations in {Country}?"
9. "List some essential tips for solo travelers."
10. "What are the top hiking trails in {Region}?"

Music and Entertainment Prompts

1. "Discuss the impact of {Artist} on the music industry."
2. "How has {Genre} evolved over the decades?"
3. "Create a list of must-watch movies for a {Genre} enthusiast."
4. "Explain the narrative structure of {Movie/Play/Book}."
5. "Generate a plot for a romantic comedy movie."
6. "What are some fundamental elements of {Music Genre}?"
7. "Discuss the cultural significance of {Movie/Play/Book}."
8. "Give me a breakdown of the thematic elements in {Album/Song}."
9. "List the top 10 timeless classic rock songs."
10. "What are some iconic movie quotes?"

Eco-Friendly Living Prompts

1. "How can I reduce my carbon footprint?"
2. "What are some tips for creating a minimalist lifestyle?"
3. "Provide a guide on how to start composting at home."
4. "What are some eco-friendly alternatives to everyday items?"
5. "Explain the benefits of using renewable energy."
6. "What are some ways to save water at home?"
7. "How to create a zero-waste kitchen?"
8. "Discuss the impact of fast fashion on the environment."
9. "What are some plant-based recipes?"
10. "How to create an eco-friendly home office?"

Start-up and Entrepreneurship Prompts

1. "What are some key considerations when starting a business?"
2. "Explain the Lean Startup methodology."
3. "What are some strategies for effective networking?"
4. "Provide a guide on how to write a business plan."
5. "What are some effective marketing strategies for a new business?"
6. "Discuss the pros and cons of bootstrapping vs. venture capital."
7. "What are some key performance indicators for {Business Type}?"
8. "How to pitch a business idea to investors?"
9. "What are some tips for managing a remote team?"
10. "Explain the concept of product-market fit."

Art and Design Prompts

1. "Discuss the influence of {Artist} on modern art."
2. "What are some principles of good web design?"
3. "Generate a color palette for a calming bedroom."
4. "What are some tips for improving my drawing skills?"
5. "Discuss the history and evolution of {Design Style}."
6. "How can I create an engaging poster for {Event}?"
7. "What are some fundamentals of photography?"
8. "Create a mood board for a coastal-themed living room."
9. "Explain the use of light and shadow in visual arts."
10. "What are some tips for DIY home decor?"

Gardening and Outdoor Prompts

1. "What are some low-maintenance plants for a beginner gardener?"
2. "Explain the process of composting and its benefits."
3. "How to create a pollinator-friendly garden?"
4. "What are some tips for organic gardening?"
5. "How can I design a small-space balcony garden?"
6. "What are some fruit trees suitable for backyard planting?"
7. "Explain the process of hydroponic gardening."
8. "Create a seasonal garden maintenance checklist."
9. "What are some natural ways to repel pests?"
10. "How to grow herbs indoors?"

Culture and History Prompts

1. "What are some important historical events that shaped {Country}?"
2. "Discuss the cultural significance of {Cultural Practice} in {Country/Region}."
3. "Explain the evolution of democracy in ancient Greece."
4. "What impact did the Renaissance have on art and culture?"
5. "Discuss the causes and effects of {Historical Event}."
6. "How has {Cultural Phenomenon} evolved over time?"
7. "What are some cultural traditions unique to {Country/Region}?"
8. "What are the key principles of {Religion/Philosophy}?"
9. "Discuss the role of women in {Historical Period}."
10. "How did the Industrial Revolution change society?"

Science and Nature Prompts

1. "Explain the theory of evolution."
2. "What are some interesting animal adaptation mechanisms?"
3. "Discuss the impact of climate change on global biodiversity."
4. "How does photosynthesis work?"
5. "What are some unsolved mysteries in physics?"
6. "What are some fascinating facts about the universe?"
7. "How does the human immune system work?"
8. "Discuss the importance of conservation and sustainable living."

9. "Explain the lifecycle of a star."
10. "What are some recent breakthroughs in scientific research?"

Film and Literature Prompts

1. "Analyze the theme of {Theme} in {Movie/Book}."
2. "What are some stylistic techniques used in {Author/Director}'s work?"
3. "Create a plot for a dystopian novel."
4. "What are some common tropes in horror cinema?"
5. "Discuss the impact of {Book/Movie} on popular culture."
6. "What are some memorable characters in {Genre} literature/film?"
7. "How to write an engaging screenplay?"
8. "What makes a good mystery novel?"
9. "Discuss the evolution of science fiction in literature."
10. "What are the principles of storytelling in film?"

Remember to adapt these templates to fit your specific needs, the specific AI you're using, and its current capabilities. These are designed to be flexible and applicable to a variety of situations, so feel free to get creative with them & modify them to better suit your needs and the specific context in which you're using them. Happy prompting!

Conclusion

As we find ourselves at the tail end of this journey through the intricate world of prompt engineering, it's fitting to reflect on the transformative capacity that thoughtful prompts hold. They are much more than mere catalysts for a software program; they are our keys to unlocking a treasury of knowledge, creativity, and solutions to myriad problems.

This book has journeyed from the basics of Generative AI and large language models to the intricate craft of constructing prompts for various uses. You've gained insights into the world of AI tools, understanding the factors that influence their responses, and the many applications that exist in our rapidly digitizing world.

Yet, the magic of AI and the significance of prompts go beyond mere practicality. They open the gates to creativity and innovation in a way we haven't previously experienced. AI has become a canvas, and prompts are the paintbrushes we use to bring our ideas to life. The precision, clarity, and creativity we bring into our prompts translate directly into the richness of the responses we receive.

Exploring the nuances of AI-based tools like ChatGPT and Midjourney, you've seen firsthand how crafting the right prompts can inspire results that are not only precise but also surprising and insightful. You've learned that AI, once considered impersonal and mechanical, can be guided to produce outputs that echo humanlike creativity, thoughtfulness, and depth.

The art of asking has been explored from various angles, from the specific context of a question to the broader landscape in which AI is functioning. We've seen how context and clarity shape the AI's responses, and how iterative refinement can polish a good prompt into a great one.

By examining the pitfalls and learning opportunities from AI errors, we've come to appreciate that even in misfires, there's a chance to learn and improve. This iterative, constantly refining process mirrors our own human journey of learning and personal development.

Looking ahead to the future, it's clear that the realm of prompt engineering is just beginning to unfurl. As AI continues to evolve, so too will our prompts, growing more refined and potent. The coming years will undoubtedly bring new opportunities and challenges alike, but equipped with the knowledge from this book, you are more than ready to navigate the future of AI and prompt engineering.

Finally, we've left you with a compendium of prompt templates. Consider these templates as the launch pad for your creativity - a place to start and branch out from. Each prompt is an invitation to engage in a dynamic, thought-provoking interaction with AI.

In a world that grows more interconnected each day, the art of asking – of crafting the right prompts – is a skill that will only grow in relevance. Whether you're seeking to generate creative content, solve complex problems, or simply learn, the power of the perfect prompt cannot be overstated.

Thank you for embarking on this journey with us, and may you carry these lessons forward as you continue to explore, question, and create. The art of asking is yours to master.